# Tapas Cookb

*Learn How to Prepare Authentic Tapas and Traditional Spanish Food at Home*

**By**

**Adele Tyler**

# Table of Contents

# Introduction

It is the tradition of enjoying tapas as a feature of Spanish cuisine that is well known throughout the world. Today, bars and restaurants around the world, ranging from the conventional to the avant-garde, recreate this culinary practice.

The word "Tapa" literally means "Cover" or "Coaster." Tapas are a type of appetizer and bite-sized morsels consumed with an alcoholic beverage, more often than not, before or between meals.

In Castilla, a historical region in Spain, men frequently went to pubs where red wine was the most prominent drink, according to the popular tales and old legends. For wine flies and other flying bugs, pubs and wine barrels were an appealing location. To stop flies drowning in the wine, the tradition of covering a bottle of wine with a "tapa" became a must.

In order to avoid drunkenness and corruption, the King of Spain, around the same time, forbade all pubs within his Kingdom to serve beer or wine unless followed by a limited quantity of food. Over the coaster, called tapa, the required portion of snack was served, and the food item itself became popular as a tapa.

Tapas were on the house with each beverage during this time. Classic tapas include chorizo, jamón and a slice of Spanish omelet, and olives. Tapas stay free for any drink in most of the cities in southern Spain. Pinchos are named as a substitute name for the small stick put through the tapas in the north and the Basque country.

One claim about the roots of Spanish tapas is that once King Alfonso X of Castile fell ill. He got recovered by drinking wine and consuming tapas between meals, and when he recovered, he requested all the wine served in inns to be supplemented by food from that moment on.

There is another royal legend surrounding tapas. Apparently, at a tavern in Cadiz, Alfonso XIII was given his wine with a slice of ham to shield it from the sand on the beach. He liked the thought, so he ordered the cover for another bottle of wine or 'tapa.'

Over the course of years, the definition of tapas has shifted. Any small quantity of food which is appropriate to complement a drink is now called a tapa, according to the official Spanish dictionary. Tapas are often accompanied with beer in Andalucia, and those in Catalonia favor vermouth. Tapas are being reinvented by modern trendy restaurants and bars and are now served as a whole meal consisting of several small dishes. Tapas are now not served in these restaurants with vermouth or barrel wine rather with sophisticated drinks or pricey wine.

Needless to mention, the tapa has grown into something much, much more nuanced since the 19th century. Although the timeless classics are still served by many traditional tapas bars in Spain, the tapas movement is constantly emerging as an emblem of the culinary identity of Spain.

Modern and creative food bars, particularly in metropolitan cities, are becoming increasingly popular throughout the world. Classic ingredients such as grilled meats, ham, and regional cheeses, paired with out-of-the-box ingredients such as fruit caramelized onions or compotes, are available in these nouvelle-styled gastro bars. There are also several international-fusion tapas bars, including mini hamburgers, Mexican-style tapas, and sushi tapas that combine flavors and styles from abroad.

While tapas differ greatly from region to region, from basic to intricate and conventional to nouvelle, one aspect remains consistent: in a communal and joyous environment, tapas are to be enjoyed with friends and relatives. While it is no longer "law" to serve a free tapa for any alcoholic drink, the practice still remains true in some places like Granada.

Some classic tapa dishes include chopitos, which are deep-fried baby squid, Gambas al Ajillo, which is garlic shrimp, Tortilla Espanola, which is a potato and egg dish, and patatas Bravas which is roasted potatoes with rojo sauce.

The following chapters of this book will include fish, meat, and vegetable-based Tapa recipes. In the end, there will be a chapter dedicated to famous Spanish dishes.

# Chapter 1: Fish Special Tapa Recipes

Fish is a low-fat, high-protein food that offers a variety of health benefits. In fact, white-fleshed fish are lower in fat than any source of animal protein, and omega-3 fatty acids or "good" fats are high in oily fish. Since no large quantities of these vital nutrients can be provided by the human body, fish are an essential part of the diet. Even the "bad" fats typically present in red meat, called omega-6 fatty acids, are low in fish. Let's get into the tapa recipes for fish.

**Seafood Paella**

Main Ingredient: Monkfish

Total time: 1 hour 50 minutes

Serving: 8 persons

**Ingredients:**

- 2 tbsp. olive oil
- 20-24 king prawns, raw
- 500g monkfish, cut into pieces
- 500g paella rice
- 1 onion, finely chopped
- 4 garlic cloves, sliced
- Pinch of saffron
- 2 tsp. smoked paprika
- 200g canned tomatoes, chopped
- 100g frozen peas
- 500g mussels, cleaned

- Handful parsley leaves, chopped
- 100g frozen baby broad beans

**For the stock**

- 1 onion, chopped
- 1 tbsp. olive oil
- 200g canned tomatoes, chopped
- 1 chicken stock cube
- 6 garlic cloves, chopped
- 1 star anise

**Method:**

1. Peel and de-vein the prawns.
2. Put the heads and shells in the fridge.
3. Cook tomatoes, onion, prawn shells and heads, and garlic in oil over medium-high heat for 3 minutes.
4. Boil star anise and stock cube in 2 liters of water for 30 minutes.
5. Blend the boiled mixture and strain finely.
6. Cook the monkfish in oil for a few minutes on each side and remove.
7. Fry onions for 4-5 minutes.
8. Add rice and cook for 30 seconds.
9. Add paprika, garlic, and saffron, and cook for another 30 seconds.
10. Add tomatoes and 1.5 liters of the fish stock.
11. Cook for 10 minutes.
12. Add monkfish, mussels, prawns, broad beans, and peas.

13. Cover the pan with foil.

14. Cook for 10-15 minutes.

15. Sprinkle with parsley and serve.

---

**Simmered Squid**

Main Ingredient: Squid

Total time: 1 hour 50 minutes

Serving: 4 persons

**Ingredients:**

- 1 kg prepared squid and tentacles, cut into thick rings
- 1 tbsp. olive oil
- 2 onions, chopped
- 1 pinch of chili flakes
- 3 garlic cloves, sliced
- 1 tsp. fennel seed
- 1 tbsp. rosemary, chopped
- 3 bay leaves
- 1 pinch of sugar
- 400g can tomato, chopped
- 3 tbsp. red wine vinegar
- 2ooml red wine

**Method:**

1. Cook onions, squid, and garlic in a pan for 2 minutes.
2. Add the dry ingredients and cook for 15 minutes.
3. Add the vinegar and tomatoes and cook for 1 minute.

4. Pour over red wine.

5. Add seasoning.

6. Cook at low for 1 hour.

7. Drizzle with olive oil.

8. Sprinkle coriander and orange zest and serve.

## Clams with Serrano Ham and Sherry

Main Ingredient: Clams

Total time: 20 minutes

Serving: 4 persons

**Ingredients:**

- ½ onion, chopped
- 1 tbsp. olive oil
- 500g fresh clams, rinsed
- Handful of parsley, chopped
- 2 garlic cloves, chopped
- 50g Serrano ham
- 100ml fino sherry

**Method:**

1. Cook onions in oil for 5-7 minutes in a covered pan.

2. Cook garlic and ham with the onion for 1 min.

3. Add sherry and clam and cook for 6-7 minutes.

4. Serve sprinkled with parsley.

# Garlic Shrimp with Lemon and Parsley

Main Ingredient: Shrimp

Total time: 15 minutes

Serving: 4 persons

## Ingredients:

- 2 tbsp. extra virgin Spanish olive oil
- 15 jumbo shrimp, peeled and de-veined
- 4 cloves of garlic, thinly sliced
- 1/2 lemon thinly sliced
- 1/4 cup white wine
- Fresh parsley, minced
- Black pepper
- Sea salt
- Crunchy baguette to serve
- Smoked paprika

## Method:

1. Season the shrimps with black pepper, sea salt, and some smoked paprika.
2. Heat 2 tablespoons of extra virgin oil over medium-high heat in a pan.
3. Put the garlic in the pan.
4. After a few seconds, add the shrimps with the seasoned side down.
5. Flip after a minute.
6. Add the wine, lemon, and half parsley.
7. Cook for a minute and a half and remove.

8. Garnish with parsley and serve with bread.

---

**Spanish Prawns, Peppers, and Aioli**

Main Ingredient: Prawns

Total time: 45 minutes

Serving: 2 persons

**Ingredients:**

- 1 ½ lemons, ½ juiced
- 2 peppers, seeded and cut into large pieces
- 4 garlic cloves, 1 sliced
- 1 onion, cut into 8 pieces
- 200g cooking chorizo sausages, halved
- Olive oil
- 2 tsp. thyme leaves
- 1 tbsp. sherry vinegar
- 2 tsp. sweet smoked paprika
- 150g mayonnaise
- 16 shell-on king prawns, raw

**Method:**

1. Heat the oven to 200° C with the fan.
2. Mix quartered lemons, peppers, garlic, onion, chorizo, 1½ tbsp. olive oil, thyme, vinegar, and 1½ tsp. paprika with seasoning.
3. Roast for 25 minutes.
4. Remove the unsliced garlic from the oven tray.
5. Add the prawns and put them back in the oven.

6. Roast for 5-10 minutes.

7. Mash the garlic cloves.

8. Mix garlic with mayonnaise, lemon juice, and remaining paprika.

9. Serve with garlicky aioli.

---

## Stuffed Fried Sardines

Main Ingredient: Sardine

Total time: 40 minutes

Serving: 4 persons

**Ingredients:**

- 1 1/2 tbsp. lemon juice
- 2 tbsp. raisins, chopped
- 1 scallion, minced
- 1 tbsp. dry fine bread crumbs
- 1 tbsp. parsley, chopped
- 1/4 cup serrano ham, finely chopped
- 1/2 tsp. fennel, ground
- 16 sardines — spines removed, butterflied
- Salt and ground pepper
- All-purpose flour
- 1 tbsp. water
- 2 large eggs
- Extra-virgin olive oil for frying

**Method:**

1. Mix raisins with ground fennel, scallion, lemon juice, parsley, chopped ham, and bread crumbs.

2. Season with salt and pepper.

3. Fill one side of sardines with filling.

4. Close the fish and press firmly.

5. Beat the eggs with water.

6. Coat sardines with flour and then egg mixture.

7. Coat with flour again.

8. Fry sardines for 2 minutes per side over medium-high heat.

9. Drain fish on paper towels.

10. Serve with mesclun salad and lemon wedges.

## Fried Calamari with Cilantro Aioli and Tabasco

Main Ingredient: Squid

Total time: 20 minutes

Serving: 2 persons

**Ingredients:**

- 1/2 cup all-purpose flour
- 1 pound calamari, tentacles cut into half-inch rings
- 1/4 cup cornstarch
- 1/2 tsp. black pepper
- 1/2 tsp. salt
- 1/2 tsp. paprika

**For the Tabasco and Honey Drizzle:**

- Tabasco sauce
- 1 1/2 tbsp. honey

**For the Cilantro Aioli:**

- 1/2 cup cilantro leaves
- 3/4 cup mayo
- 1/2 tsp. salt
- 1/2 tsp. cumin
- 1/4 tsp. black pepper
- 1 tsp. lime juice and zest

**Method:**

1. Heat the oil in a saucepan over medium flame.
2. Coat calamari with cornstarch, flour, spices.
3. Fry calamari for 3-4 minutes, or until crispy and golden.
4. Mix honey and Tabasco.
5. Combine ingredients for aioli.
6. Serve calamari with sauces.

---

**Clams in Green Sauce**

Main Ingredient: Clams

Total time: 20 minutes

Serving: 5 persons

**Ingredients:**

- 8 oz. white wine

- 1 1/2 pounds clams, cleaned
- 4 garlic cloves, minced
- 1 tbsp. olive oil
- 1 small onion, chopped
- 2 tbsp. flour
- 1/4 tsp. salt
- 2 tbsp. flat-leaf parsley, chopped

**Method:**

1. Put clams in a medium saucepan.
2. Add the half wine.
3. Add water to cover clams.
4. Bring the mix to a boil.
5. Simmer until the clams open and set aside.
6. Fry onions.
7. Add garlic after 3-4 minutes.
8. Reduce heat when onions become transparent.
9. Add the flour.
10. Add wine and clam residue while stirring.
11. Add clams.
12. Cook for 3-4 minutes.
13. Sprinkle parsley.
14. Serve with slices of baguette.

**Grilled Cajun Prawns**

Main Ingredient: Prawns

Total time: 15 minutes

Serving: 4 persons

**Ingredients:**

- 40g cheddar cheese
- 800g sweet potatoes, sliced
- 16 large shelled Australian green banana prawns
- 1 tbsp. Cajun seasoning
- 3 garlic cloves, minced
- Olive oil
- 1 lemon
- 15g fresh thyme
- 1 capsicum, green and red each, de-seeded and chopped
- 2 sticks of celery, sliced
- 5 spring onions, sliced
- 1 handful frozen sweet corn
- ½ red chili, sliced
- 1 tsp. sweet smoked paprika

**Method:**

1. Boil potatoes with salt.
2. Put prawns, garlic, Cajun seasoning, thyme sprigs, and 1 tbsp. oil.
3. Keep the heat on high for a few minutes.
4. Place under the grill for the top to be crispy.
5. Fry peppers.

6. Add spring onions, salt, pepper, celery, chili, paprika, and sweet corn.

7. Mash potatoes.

8. Add cheese to potatoes.

9. Add vegetables to mash.

10. Serve it with lemon wedges and prawns.

## Garden-Fresh Seafood Cocktail

Main Ingredient: Shrimp

Total time: 1 hour 15 minutes

Serving: 6 persons

**Ingredients:**

- 8 oz. refrigerated jumbo lump crabmeat, drained
- 3/4 pound cooked shrimp, peeled and de-veined
- 3 celery ribs, chopped
- 1 sweet orange pepper, chopped
- 1 cucumber, peeled, seeded, and chopped
- 2 plum tomatoes, seeded and chopped
- 1-2 jalapeno peppers, seeded and chopped
- 1/2 cup red onion, chopped
- 1/4 cup cilantro, minced
- 1 tbsp. olive oil
- 3 tbsp. lime juice
- 2-1/4 tsp. adobo seasoning

**Method:**

1. Mix oil, adobo seasoning, and lime juice.

2. Combine the rest of the ingredients.

3. Drizzle sauce over shrimp mixture.

4. Refrigerate 1-hour tossing thrice in between and serve.

## Griddled Octopus with Potatoes and Olives

Main Ingredient: Octopus

Total time: 1 hour 40 minutes

Serving: 6 persons

**Ingredients:**

- 1 bay leaf
- 1kg octopus, prepared and rinsed
- 2 thyme sprigs
- 1 carrot, chopped
- 2 onions, chopped
- 1 garlic bulb, cut horizontally
- 1 celery stick, chopped
- ½ tsp. coriander, ground
- 10 large potatoes
- ½ tsp. whole peppercorns
- 5 mint leaves, chopped
- Paprika to taste
- 1 lemon zest, grated
- 2 tbsp. flat-leaf parsley, chopped
- 10 green olives, pitted and sliced

**Method:**

1. Add the octopus with remaining ingredients except potatoes, mint leaves, paprika, and 1 onion in a pan full of cold water.
2. Bring it to a boil.
1. Keep it on low heat for 45 minutes.
2. Remove the octopus.
3. Add water to the residue and cook for 15 minutes.
4. Thickly slice potatoes and add to bowl with some olive oil.
5. Cut the octopus into 8cm pieces.
6. Brush with olive oil.
7. Char it on the griddle on high heat.
8. Mix the rest of the ingredients with the potatoes.
9. Add octopus on top.
10. Sprinkle with parsley and olives and serve.

---

### Flash-fried Prawns with Chili

Main Ingredient: Prawns

Total time: 15 minutes

Serving: 7 persons

**Ingredients:**

- 300g prawn, raw and butterflied
- 2 tbsp. extra-virgin olive oil
- 2 garlic cloves, chopped
- 1 lemon zest and juice

- 1 tsp. chili flakes
- 2 tbsp. flat-leaf parsley, chopped

**Method:**

1. Coat prawns with seasoning and set aside.
2. Fry garlic in a pan over medium heat for a few minutes.
3. Add chili and prawns when garlic browns on high heat.
4. Toss prawns in the pan.
5. Add lemon juice after 1 minute.
6. Toss prawns for another minute.
7. Sprinkle parsley and over the lemon zest.
8. Serve prawns with crusty bread.

---

### Smoked Cod Fritters

Main Ingredient: Cod

Total time: 20 minutes

Serving: 3 persons

**Ingredients:**

- 1 onion, grated
- 300ml milk
- 500g smoked cod fillet, de-boned
- 1 lemon zest
- 2 large starchy potatoes, diced
- ½ a bunch of dill, chopped
- 1 egg

- 3 tbsp. plain flour
- Lemon wedges

**Method:**

1. Put the onion in a pan with milk to cover.
2. Cook for 5 minutes.
3. Add the fish and cook for 4 more minutes and remove.
4. Add the potatoes to the pan. Cook until tender.
5. Mash the potatoes, fish, lemon zest, flour, dill, and egg and add seasoning.
6. Make balls of tbsp. mixture.
7. Refrigerate for 30 minutes.
8. Heat oil covering 1 cm of a frying pan.
9. Cook the fritters until crispy.
10. Serve with lemon wedges.

---

**Saucy Shrimp and Clams with Wild Mushrooms**

Main Ingredient: Clams

Total time: 20 minutes

Serving: 3 persons

**Ingredients:**

- 1/2 cup extra-virgin olive oil
- 1/2 pound shiitake mushrooms, thickly sliced
- Salt and ground pepper
- 1 large hot red chile, seeded and chopped
- 24 littleneck clams, cleaned

- 1 1/4 cups fruity dry white wine
- 1 pound shrimp, shelled and de-veined
- Crusty bread
- 1 bunch of scallions, light green and white part

**Method:**

1. Cook shiitake mushrooms in the oil over high heat tossing around for 5 minutes.
2. Season with salt and pepper.
3. Put in chile and scallions and cook for 2 minutes.
4. Put in the wine and clams and wine and cook for 4 minutes.
5. Add in shrimp and cook for 4 minutes.
6. Serve with crusty bread.

## Spanish Shellfish Soup

Main Ingredient: Shrimp

Total time: 40 minutes

Serving: 6 persons

**Ingredients:**

- 1/2 cup olive oil
- 1 cup rice
- 1 yellow onion, chopped
- 1 tomato, chopped
- 1 carrot, chopped
- 2 bay leaves
- 12 littleneck clams

- 1 fish head for broth
- 1 lb. shrimps (20 to 25 per lb.)
- Salt and pepper to taste
- 1 cup white wine

**Method:**

1. Cook bay leaves, clams, and fish head in 4 cups of water for 15 minutes.
2. Add shrimps and cook for 5 minutes.
3. Sauté tomato, onion, and carrot in oil until onion are translucent.
4. Add the wine and cook for 5 minutes.
5. Add the wine-vegetable mixture to a pot.
6. Strain the broth.
7. Add to pot and stir.
8. Set the meat aside from fish heads and shrimp.
9. Cook the pot on medium-high heat.
10. Put in rice when soup boils.
11. Cook on medium-high heat for 15 minutes.
12. Season with salt and pepper.
13. Put the meat back in and serve.

**Party Squid and Harissa Mayo**

Main Ingredient: Squid

Total time: 1 hour 20 minutes

Serving: 8 persons

**Ingredients:**

- 3 sprigs of flowering oregano
- 3 lemons
- 2 tbsp. fennel seeds
- 300g plain flour
- 1 tsp. white pepper
- 12 medium squids, prepared with tentacles
- 1 garlic clove, minced
- Fresh flat-leaf parsley
- 3 tbsp. Hellmann's Mayonnaise
- 1½ tsp. rose water
- 4 tsp. harissa paste
- 1 ½ tsp. sea salt

**Method:**

1. Mix garlic, ½ tsp. sea salt, juice, and zest of ½ lemon, half harissa, and mayo together.
2. Gently mix rosewater and remaining harissa.
3. Process oregano flowers, fennel, pepper, and remaining salt.
4. Combine the mixture with flour in a bowl.
5. Slice the tubes of squid.
6. Make crisscross cuts.
7. Coat with flour mixture.
8. Deep fry in oil for 3 to 4 minutes.
9. Coat parsley with the flour mix and fry for a few seconds.

10. Coat slices of lemon with the flour mix and fry for 1 minute.

11. Serve squid with parsley, fried lemon, lemon wedges, and harissa mayo.

---

## Ginger-Tuna Kabobs

Main Ingredient: Tuna

Total time: 1 hour

Serving: 4 persons

**Ingredients:**

- 1/4 cup soy sauce
- 1 pound tuna steaks, chopped into 16 cubes
- 2 tbsp. rice vinegar
- 1 tsp. pepper
- 1 tbsp. sesame seeds
- 2 tbsp. canola oil
- 16 pickled ginger slices
- 1/2 cup wasabi mayonnaise

**Method:**

1. Coat tuna with vinegar and soy sauce.
2. Cover and refrigerate for 30 minutes.
3. Drain tuna and pat dry.
4. Add pepper and sesame seeds to tuna.
5. Cook tuna in a pan until the center is medium-rare.
6. Add a tuna cube and ginger slice to each skewer.
7. Serve skewers with wasabi mayonnaise.

# Baked Oysters with Tasso Cream

Main Ingredient: Oysters

Total time: 1 hour 10 minutes

Serving: 4 persons

## Ingredients:

- 1/4 cup butter, melted
- 4 slices white bread
- 1/8 tsp. salt
- 3 ounces Tasso ham, finely chopped
- 1/8 tsp. pepper
- 2 tbsp. sweet onion, chopped
- 2 cups heavy whipping cream
- 1 garlic clove, minced
- 2 dashes Louisiana-style hot sauce
- 1 dozen fresh shell oysters, scrubbed
- Salt and pepper to taste

## Method:

1. Preheat oven to 300° C.
2. Bake bread for 8-10 minutes on both sides.
3. Make bread crumbs in a processor.
4. Add in salt, melted butter, and pepper.
5. Cook ham until lightly browned over medium heat.
6. Add in garlic and onion.
7. Cook for 1-2 minutes.

8. Add cream.

9. Boil the mixture until half remains.

10. Add salt, hot sauce, and pepper.

11. Heat oven to 350°C.

12. Shuck oysters.

13. Bake oysters sprinkled with bread crumbs for 8-10 minutes.

14. Serve with sauce.

---

## Teriyaki Salmon Bundles

Main Ingredient: Salmon

Total time: 50 minutes

Serving: 5-6 persons

**Ingredients:**

- 1/2 tsp. grated lemon zest
- 4 tbsp. reduced-sodium teriyaki sauce, divided
- 2 tbsp. lemon juice
- 17.3 oz. frozen puff pastry, thawed
- 1-1/4 pounds salmon fillet, cut into 1-inch cubes
- 2/3 cup orange marmalade

**Method:**

1. Preheat oven to 400°C.

2. Mix half teriyaki sauce, lemon juice, and zest.

3. Coat salmon with mixture and set it aside for 20 minutes.

4. Drain salmon.

5. Cut sheets into half-inch wide strips.

6. Cut strips horizontally in half.

7. Overlap 2 pastry strips in an X shape.

8. Wrap salmon in each strip and seal.

9. Bake on a greased baking sheet for 18-20 minutes.

10. Mix remaining teriyaki and marmalade.

11. Serve salmon bundle with sauce.

## Asian Shrimp Pancakes

Main Ingredient: Shrimp

Total time: 30 minutes

Serving: 6-8 persons

**Ingredients:**

- 3/4 tsp. salt

- 2 garlic cloves, minced

- 2 large eggs

- 2 tsp. toasted sesame oil

- 3/4 cup water

- 1 cup all-purpose flour

- 1/2 sweet red pepper, chopped

- 6 green onions, sliced

- 1/2 pound shrimp halved lengthwise, peeled, de-veined, and cooked

- Sriracha chili sauce, wasabi mayonnaise, or fresh cilantro leaves

**Method:**

1. Mix garlic with salt.

2. Add water, green onions, pepper, eggs, and oil.

3. Add flour and mix.

4. Put mixture by tablespoons over a greased griddle on medium-high heat.

5. Cook until golden brown on both sides.

6. Add a shrimp half on all pancake tops.

7. Serve with toppings.

# Chapter 2: Meat Special Tapa Recipes

Meat is one of the most important, healthy, and preferred food products available to the masses, which helps to satisfy most of their body requirements. In human evolution, it has played a critical role and is an imperative feature of a well-balanced diet. It is a healthy source of vitamin A and B-complex vitamins, proteins, zinc, iron, selenium, and phosphorus. Let's get into the tapa recipes for meat.

**Ham and Cheese Croquetas**

Main Ingredient: Pork

Total time: 1 hour 25 minutes

Serving: 4-6 persons

**Ingredients:**

- ½ small onion, chopped
- 25g butter
- 50g plain flour
- 140g smoked ham, diced
- 250ml milk
- 50g mature cheddar, grated
- 2 tbsp. double cream
- 1 tsp. Dijon mustard
- 50g gruyère, grated
- For the coating
- 50g plain flour
- 2 large eggs

- 140g fine dried breadcrumbs
- For the tomato chili jam
- 1 long red chili, chopped
- 300g ripe tomatoes, chopped
- 1 small red onion, chopped
- 100g demerara sugar
- 4 garlic cloves, crushed
- 100ml red wine vinegar

**Method:**

1. Fry onions for 3 minutes in butter.
2. Add flour and cook for 30 seconds.
3. Slowly add milk and cook for 5 minutes, stirring constantly.
4. Add the cheese, ham, mustard, seasoning, and cream.
5. Cook for 1 minute.
6. Let cool and refrigerate for 4 hours.
7. Make 24 balls each of 1 tablespoon mixture.
8. Beat eggs.
9. Roll balls in flour.
10. Coat with egg.
11. Coat with breadcrumbs.
12. Refrigerate for 30 minutes.
13. Cook ingredients for tomato chili jam for 1-hour, stirring continuously.
14. Heat saucepan with one-third full sunflower oil.
15. Cook croquettes for 1 and half minutes.

16. Serve with the chili jam.

---

## Smoky Albondigas

Main Ingredient: Beef

Total time: 40 minutes

Serving: 4 persons

**Ingredients:**

- 4 white bread crust-less slices, cut into small pieces
- 6 tbsp. milk
- 400g beef mince
- 400g pork mince
- 1 garlic clove, minced
- Parsley, chopped
- 1 egg
- ½ tsp. smoked paprika

**For Tomato Sauce**

- 2 garlic cloves, sliced
- 200ml red wine
- 2 × 400g tins tomatoes, chopped
- Smoked paprika

**Method:**

1. Put bread in a bowl.
2. Add milk.
3. Put in garlic, mince, parsley, smoked paprika egg, and seasoning.

4. Roll mixture into small balls.

5. Fry meatballs until brown and remove.

6. Fry the garlic for a few minutes.

7. Add wine and let it all be absorbed.

8. Add the smoked paprika, seasoning, and tomatoes.

9. Cook for 10 minutes.

10. Put in the meatballs and cook on low for 20 minutes and serve.

## Chorizo-Filled Dates Wrapped in Bacon

Main Ingredient: Bacon

Total time: 20 minutes

Serving: 4-6 persons

**Ingredients:**

- 24 Medjool dates, pitted
- 1 Spanish chorizo sausage, skin removed
- 12 bacon slices, halved horizontally

**Method:**

1. Cut the chorizo pieces in thirds.

2. Now, halve the pieces lengthwise.

3. Cut each half into 4 strips vertically.

4. Put a chorizo stick into each date.

5. Fold a bacon strip around each date.

6. Secure bacon with a toothpick.

7. Sauté the dates in a skillet for 10 minutes, tossing in between.

8. Drain and serve hot.

---

## Mushroom Croquettes

Main Ingredient: Mushrooms

Total time: 1 hour 15 minutes

Serving: 4 persons

**Ingredients:**

- 1 ½ cups bread crumbs
- ½ onion, diced
- ¼ cup olive oil, divided
- 2 garlic cloves, minced
- ½ cup flour
- 215 grams mushrooms, finely diced
- 2 ¾ cups unsweetened plant-based milk, divided
- ½ tsp. salt, plus more for the mushrooms
- ½ cup vegetable stock
- Pepper to taste

**Method:**

1. Fry onions until transparent in a pan over medium heat.
2. Add the garlic and cook until fragrant.
3. Set aside the mixture.
4. Fry mushrooms until browned.
5. Season with salt and pepper.
6. Add mushrooms to the onion and garlic mixture.

7. Combine 1 ¾ cups of the plant milk with the vegetable stock in a bowl.

8. Sift flour in an oiled pan in small portions.

9. Cook for a minute or two.

10. Add the milk-water mixture slowly and cook until the sauce thickens.

11. Set aside and add ½ teaspoon salt, mushrooms, pepper, garlic, and onion.

12. Once cool, put on plastic wrap and refrigerate for 30 minutes.

13. Add the remaining cup of plant milk in one bowl.

14. Put breadcrumbs in another bowl.

15. Shape a teaspoon of the filling into a log.

16. Roll it in breadcrumbs.

17. Dip it into the milk and cover with the breadcrumbs again.

18. Deep fry until golden brown and serve.

---

## Chicken and Chorizo Paella

Main Ingredient: Chicken

Total time: 50 minutes

Serving: 4 persons

**Ingredients:**

- 1 onion, chopped
- 2 cloves of garlic, sliced
- 1 carrot, chopped
- 70 g quality chorizo, chopped

- ½ a bunch of flat-leaf parsley, chopped
- 2 chicken thighs, bone out, and chopped
- 1 tsp. sweet smoked paprika
- 1 tbsp. tomato purée
- 1 red pepper, chopped
- 1 organic chicken stock cube, chopped
- 100g frozen peas
- 1 lemon
- 30g paella rice
- 200g frozen cooked prawns, peeled

**Method:**

1. Fry the onion, garlic, carrot, chorizo, parsley stalks, paprika, and chicken in a paella pan for around 5 minutes.
2. Add the pepper and cook for 5 minutes.
3. Add tomato purée, stock cube, and rice and stir.
4. Add 750ml boiling water, salt, and pepper.
5. Cook for 15 minutes on low.
6. Add peas and prawns, and cook for 5 minutes.
7. Add seasoning and parsley leaves to the paella.
8. Serve with lemon wedges.

**Steak and Blue Cheese Bruschetta with Jam**

Main Ingredient: Beef

Total time: 55 minutes

Serving: 4 persons

## Ingredients:

- 1 large sweet onion, sliced
- 5 tbsp. olive oil, divided
- 1 cup grape tomatoes, halved
- 1/4 tsp. ground pepper, divided
- 1/2 tsp. kosher salt, divided
- 6 oz. cream cheese, softened
- 3 garlic cloves, minced
- 3/4 cup crumbled blue cheese
- 16 slices French bread baguette
- 1-1/2 tsp. Montreal steak seasoning
- 2 (8 oz.) beef rib-eye steaks
- 2 tbsp. balsamic vinegar

## Method:

1. Preheat oven to 400°C.
2. Sauté onions in oil until softened.
3. Cook for 25-30 minutes.
4. Coat tomatoes with 1/4 teaspoon salt, 1 tablespoon oil, and 1/8 teaspoon pepper.
5. Add tomatoes to a 15x10x1 inch pan.
6. Roast for 10-15 minutes.
7. Mix tomatoes with onion.
8. Mix blue cheese, cream cheese, remaining salt and pepper, and garlic.
9. Brush bread slices oil.
10. Grill bread 1-2 minutes per side.

11. Sprinkle steaks with steak seasoning.

12. Grill over 3-5 minutes per side over medium heat.

13. Spread cheese mixture on toasts.

14. Top toasts with onion and steak mixture.

15. Drizzle with vinegar and serve.

---

### Sherry Braised Chorizo Sausages

Main Ingredient: Pork

Total time: 45 minutes

Serving: 8 persons

**Ingredients:**

- 2 (190g) packs cooking chorizo sausages
- 1 tbsp. olive oil
- 2 large roasted red peppers, sliced
- 2 tbsp. light brown soft sugar
- 200ml amontillado sherry
- Fresh parsley, chopped

**For the chickpeas**

- 6 tbsp. extra-virgin olive oil
- 6 garlic cloves, peeled
- 3 (400g) tins chickpeas, rinsed
- Sea salt flakes
- 1½ lemon zest and juice

**Method:**

1. Preheat the oven to 161°C on fan.

2. Wrap the garlic in foil.

3. Roast for 15-20 minutes.

4. Cook the sausages over medium-high heat for 5-7 minutes.

5. Add peppers and cook for 5 minutes.

6. Add brown sugar and sherry and mix.

7. Cook for 1 minute and in the oven cook for 25 minutes.

8. Cook chickpeas in oil for 2-3 minutes.

9. Add 200ml water and cook for 3-4 minutes.

10. Mash chickpeas and add 3 tbsp. oil.

11. Add crushed lemon zest, mashed roasted garlic, lemon juice, salt, and pepper.

12. Top chickpeas with the sherry sauce and sausages.

13. Serve sprinkled with parsley.

## Andalusian-Style Chicken

Main Ingredient: Chicken

Total time: 40 minutes

Serving: 4 persons

**Ingredients:**

- ½ chicken stock cube
- 1 large pinch of saffron
- 2 tbsp. olive oil
- 2 large chicken breasts, bite-sized pieces
- 1 onion, sliced
- 1 large pinch of ground cinnamon

- 2 tbsp. sherry vinegar
- 1 red chili, chopped
- 1 tbsp. clear honey
- 1 tbsp. raisins
- 6 cherry tomatoes, quartered
- A handful of coriander, chopped
- Crusty bread
- 25g toasted almonds

**Method:**

1. Crumble chicken stock in 100ml boiling water.
2. Add the saffron to soak in the hot stock.
3. Cook the onion until soft in oil.
4. Add the chicken.
5. Cook for a few minutes.
6. Add chili and cinnamon, and cook for a few minutes.
7. Add the vinegar, stock, honey, raisins, and tomatoes.
8. Simmer for 10 minutes.
9. Serve topped with nuts, coriander, and bread on the side.

## Lamb Meatballs with Mint

Main Ingredient: Lamb

Total time: 40 minutes

Serving: 4 persons

**Ingredients:**

- 1 egg

- 1 pound lean ground lamb
- ¼ cup dry bread crumbs
- Salt and ground pepper
- 2 tbsp. mint, chopped
- ½ cup extra-virgin olive oil
- 1 garlic clove, chopped
- 1 onion, chopped
- ½ cup dry white wine
- 1 cup tomato puree
- ½ cup beef broth

**Method:**

1. Mix egg, the lamb, bread crumbs, and half mint.
2. Season with salt and pepper.
3. Make 1-inch balls out of the mixture.
4. Fry the meatballs for 4 minutes and remove.
5. Cook garlic and onion for 8 minutes.
6. Add wine and cook for 5 minutes.
7. Add the mixture to a processor.
8. Add the remaining mint and blend.
9. Put the onion puree in a pan.
10. Add the tomato puree, broth, and meatballs and cook for 10 minutes on low heat.
11. Season with pepper and salt and serve.

---

**Chicken Empanadas**

Main Ingredient: Chicken

Total time: 30 minutes

Serving: 2-3 persons

**Ingredients:**

- 2 cups of cooked chicken, shredded
- 10 empanada disks
- 1 ½ cups of shredded Monterey Jack cheese
- 1/2 cup red bell pepper
- 4 oz. can green chilies, diced
- ½ cup of Greek yogurt
- 1 tsp. of salt
- 1 tbsp. of cumin
- ½ tsp. pepper
- 1-2 tbsp. Sriracha
- ½ tsp. of paprika
- 1 egg

**Method:**

1. Pre-heat your oven to 204°C.
2. Combine cheese, chicken, green chilies, Greek yogurt, bell pepper, cumin, paprika, sriracha, salt, and pepper.
3. Spoon 2 tablespoons of the mixture onto discs.
4. Leave ¼ inch space around the edge.
5. Brush the edges, fold, and seal.
6. Give discs an egg wash.
7. Bake for 12-15 minutes until empanadas turn golden and serve.

## Crunchy Chicken with an Herby Yoghurt Dip

Main Ingredient: Chicken

Total time: 40 minutes

Serving: 6 persons

**Ingredients:**

- 2 (200g) free-range skinless chicken breasts
- 1 lemon zest, grated
- Breadcrumbs out of 2-3 thick slices
- 1 tsp. sweet smoked paprika
- Sea salt
- Ground black pepper

**For Yoghurt Dip:**

- 1 lemon
- 4 sprigs of fresh mint, chopped
- ¼ clove of garlic, chopped
- Sea salt
- 200g natural yogurt
- Ground black pepper

**Method:**

1. Mix mint leaves, the juice from a lemon, ½ lemon grated zest, salt, and pepper in yogurt.
2. Add half of the yogurt to a bowl.
3. Cut the chicken into 2cm strips lengthwise and add to bowl.
4. Refrigerate for 30 minutes.
5. Preheat the oven to 190°C.

6. Add the breadcrumbs, paprika, lemon zest, salt, and pepper to a bowl.

7. Coat chicken with breadcrumbs.

8. Drizzle olive oil on chicken.

9. Bake for 20 to 25 minutes.

10. Serve chicken with minty yogurt and tomato salad.

### Bacon-Cheddar Potato Croquettes

Main Ingredient: Pork

Total time: 40 minutes

Serving: 10-15 persons

**Ingredients:**

- 6 bacon strips crumbled, cooked
- 4 cups cold mashed potatoes
- 1/2 cup cheddar cheese, shredded
- 1/4 cup sour cream
- 2 eggs, beaten
- 1 tbsp. chives, minced
- 1/4 tsp. pepper
- 1/2 tsp. salt
- 40 Ritz crackers, crushed
- 1 tsp. paprika
- 1/4 cup butter, melted
- Dijon-mayonnaise blend, Barbecue sauce, or ranch salad dressing

**Method:**

1. Combine all the ingredients except paprika, crackers, butter, and dipping.

2. Make balls out of 1 tablespoon mixture.

3. Coat with cracker crumbs.

4. Cover and refrigerate for 2 hours.

5. Mix paprika and butter.

6. Drizzle and mix over croquettes.

7. Bake at 375°C for 18-20 minutes.

8. Serve with dipping sauce.

## Seared Beef, Grilled Pepper and Caper Berry

Main Ingredient: Beef

Total time: 15 minutes

Serving: 6-8 persons

**Ingredients:**

- 2tbsp. olive oil
- 400g sirloin steak, fat trimmed
- 2 garlic cloves, crushed
- 12 caper berries
- 4 piquillo peppers, sliced

**Method:**

1. Season the steak with ground black pepper.

2. Brush steak with oil.

3. Mix the remaining oil with garlic.

4. Cook steak on the griddle for 3 minutes on both sides.

5. Brush steak with the garlicky oil.

6. Season with salt.

7. Rest for 5 minutes.

8. Slice the steaks into small pieces and top with a caper berry and red pepper.

9. Push the food items through a cocktail stick.

10. Drizzle oil and sprinkle pepper to serve.

---

## Pincho Ribs with Sherry Glaze

Main Ingredient: Beef

Total time: 3 hours

Serving: 8 persons

**Ingredients:**

- ½ cup smoked sweet paprika
- 1 tbsp. granulated onion
- 1 tbsp. ground red pepper
- 1 tbsp. granulated garlic
- 1 tbsp. ground cumin
- 1 tbsp. ground black pepper
- 1 tbsp. ground coriander
- 4 racks baby back ribs
- 1 tbsp. dried oregano
- ¼ cup kosher salt

Glaze

- ¾ cup dry sherry
- 1 cup honey
- ½ tsp. Sriracha chile sauce

- 2 tbsp. soy sauce
- 1 tsp. kosher salt
- 1 tbsp. tomato paste
- 2 dashes Angostura

**Method:**

1. Preheat the oven to 350°C.
2. Coat ribs with salt, paprika, onion, red pepper, garlic, cumin, black pepper, coriander, and oregano.
3. Put the ribs in a roasting pan.
4. Cover pan with foil tightly.
5. Roast for 2 hours.
6. Boil sherry, honey, soy sauce, salt, tomato paste, bitters, and Sriracha for 8 minutes.
7. Increase the heat up to 204°C.
8. Slice the racks to individual ribs.
9. Coat the ribs with glaze.
10. Cook in the upper and lower thirds portion of the oven for 15 minutes.
11. Brush the ribs halfway by the rest of the glaze and serve.

---

## Bacon-Wrapped Dates with Pecans and Goat Cheese

Main Ingredient: Pork

Total time: 30 minutes

Serving: 10 persons

**Ingredients:**

- 18 Medjool dates, pitted
- 9 slices bacon, halved
- 4 oz. goat cheese
- ¼ cup dark brown sugar
- 18 pecans, halved

**Method:**

1. Pre-heat oven to 190°C.
2. Put the oven rack in the middle.
3. Put goat cheese in the hole of the dates.
4. Place pecan in between the goat cheese and press to close.
5. Wrap half of a bacon slice around each date.
6. Secure with a toothpick.
7. Coat the dates with brown sugar.
8. Bake the dates for 10 minutes.
9. Turn the dates over.
10. Bake dates for an additional 8 minutes.
11. Broil dates for 1 minute per side.
12. Serve the dates as they are, or slice each date into pieces and serve.

---

**Petite Sausage Quiches**

Main Ingredient: Pork

Total time: 55 minutes

Serving: 6-8 persons

**Ingredients:**

- 6 oz. cream cheese, softened
- 1 cup butter, softened
- 2 cups all-purpose flour

Filling:

- 1 cup Swiss cheese, shredded
- 6 oz. bulk Italian sausage
- 1 tbsp. minced chives
- 1/2 cup half-and-half cream
- Dash cayenne pepper
- 1 large egg
- 1/4 tsp. salt

## Methods:

1. Preheat oven to 190°C.
2. Mix cream cheese, butter, and flour.
3. Make 36 balls out of the mixture.
4. Make cavities up and down the muffins.
5. Grease the muffins.
6. Cook sausage until no longer pink over medium heat and crumble.
7. Top pieces of sausages, chives, and Swiss cheese on muffins.
8. Mix cream, egg, pepper, and salt.
9. Pour into shells.
10. Bake for 28-30 minutes and serve.

## Bacon and Fontina Stuffed Mushrooms

Main Ingredient: Pork

Total time: 40 minutes

Serving: 4-6 persons

**Ingredients:**

- 1 cup fontina cheese, shredded
- 4 oz. cream cheese, softened
- 8 bacon crumbled strips, cooked
- 1/4 cup sun-dried tomatoes (oil-packed), chopped
- 4 green onions, chopped
- 3 tbsp. fresh parsley, minced
- 1 tbsp. olive oil
- 24 mushrooms, stems removed

**Method:**

1. Preheat oven to 218°C.
2. Mix all ingredients except mushrooms and olive oil.
3. Put mushroom caps evenly with stems up in an oiled 15x10x1 inch baking pan.
4. Add 1 tablespoon filling to each mushroom.
5. Drizzle the top of mushrooms with oil.
6. Bake for 9-11 minutes and serve.

## Brown Sugar-Glazed Meatballs

Main Ingredient: Pork

Total time: 55 minutes

Serving: 8-10 persons

**Ingredients:**

- 3/4 pound shrimp, peeled, deveined, uncooked, and chopped
- 1/2 cup soft bread crumbs
- 4 bacon strips, chopped
- 1 egg, beaten
- 1 tbsp. stone-ground mustard
- 1-1/2 tsp. liquid smoke
- 1-1/2 tsp. smoked paprika
- 1 tsp. salt
- 1 garlic clove, minced
- 3/4 tsp. dried oregano
- 1/2 to 1 tsp. hot pepper sauce
- 1/2 tsp. onion powder
- 1 pound ground pork

Glaze:

- 1/4 cup cider vinegar
- 1/2 cup packed brown sugar
- 4 tsp. stone-ground mustard

**Method:**

1. Preheat oven to 176°C.
2. Mix all the ingredients except pork.
3. Add pork and mix lightly.
4. Shape mixture into 1 inch balls.
5. Bake meatballs for 14-17 minutes.

6. Mix the ingredients for the glaze.

7. Add meatballs to the glaze.

8. Cook for 9-10 minutes over medium-high heat, stirring occasionally, and serve.

---

**Ham and Cheese Biscuit Stacks**

Main Ingredient: Pork

Total time: 1 hour 10 minutes

Serving: 8-10 persons

**Ingredients:**

- 1/4 cup honey
- 1/4 cup stone-ground mustard
- (6 oz. each) 4 tubes refrigerated flaky biscuits
- 1/2 cup butter
- 1/2 cup mustard (stone-ground)
- 10 slices deli ham, cut into 4 pieces
- 1/4 cup green onions, chopped
- 1/4 cup mayonnaise
- 10 Swiss cheese slices, cut into 4 pieces
- 20 ripe olives, pitted and drained
- 2-1/2 cups romaine, shredded
- 20 olives (pimiento-stuffed), drained

**Method:**

1. Pre-heat oven to 205°C.

2. Slice biscuits to make semi-circles.

3. Arrange pieces at a distance of 2 inches from each other on an ungreased pan.

4. Spread mustard on the biscuits.

5. Bake until brown for 8-10 minutes.

6. Mix green onions and butter.

7. Mix mayonnaise, mustard, and honey in another bowl.

8. Place two biscuits as two layers.

9. Put butter mixture on the lower layer.

10. Put cheese, ham, biscuit, and romaine on the top.

11. Put mustard mixture over the top layer.

12. Add olives into toothpicks.

13. Insert toothpicks into stacks and serve.

## Southwestern Pulled Pork Crostini

Main Ingredient: Pork

Total time: 6 hours 45 minutes

Serving: 6-8 persons

**Ingredients:**

- 1 boneless (2-pound) pork shoulder butt roast
- 1/2 cup lime juice
- 2 envelopes mesquite marinade mix
- 1/4 cup sugar
- 1/4 cup olive oil

**Salsa:**

- 1 cup canned black beans, drained
- 1 cup frozen corn, thawed

- 2 tbsp. olive oil
- 2 tbsp. seeded jalapeno pepper, chopped
- 1 small tomato, chopped
- 2 tbsp. lime juice
- 1 tsp. chili powder
- 1-1/2 tsp. ground cumin
- 1/4 tsp. crushed red pepper flakes
- 1/2 tsp. salt

## Sauce

- 1/8 tsp. salt
- 1/3 cup apricot preserves
- 1 can (4 oz.) green chilies, chopped

## Crostini

- 1/4 cup olive oil
- 32 slices French bread baguette
- 2/3 cup feta cheese, crumbled

## Method:

1. Put roast in a slow cooker (3 quarts.)
2. Combine lime juice, sugar, marinade mix, and oil.
3. Put mix over roast.
4. Cook on low 6-8 hours covered.
5. Combine beans, corn, jalapeno, and tomato.
6. Add oil, lime juice, and seasonings.
7. Cook sauce ingredients on low heat.
8. Preheat broiler.
9. Brush oil on bread slices.

10. Broil for 1-2 minutes 3 inches away from the heat on both sides.

11. Remove roast and let cool.

12. Shred pork.

13. Layer toasts with pork, salsa, and cheese.

14. Top toast with sauce.

15. Serve toasts with lime wedges.

# Chapter 3: Vegetable Special Tapa Recipes

Due to their minerals, vitamins, phytochemical compounds, vegetables, and dietary fiber content are important for human health. In fact, the content of antioxidant vitamins (vitamin C, vitamin A, and vitamin E) and dietary fiber play a major role in human health. Any chronic diseases such as diabetes, obesity, cancer, cardiovascular diseases, and metabolic syndrome, as well as risk factors associated with these diseases can be avoided by adequate vegetable intake.

**Kale Salad with Almonds and Serrano Ham**

Main Ingredient: Kale

Total time: 35 minutes

Serving: 2-3 persons

**Ingredients:**

- 2 tsp. vegetable oil
- 2 banana shallots, sliced
- 200g kale, leaves roughly cut
- 3 celery sticks, thinly sliced
- 4-6 slices serrano ham
- Shavings of manchego cheese

**For the almonds**

- ½ tsp. vegetable oil
- 2 tbsp. whole blanched almonds
- Sweet smoked paprika

**For the dressing**

- 2 tbsp. extra virgin olive oil

- 2 tbsp. sherry vinegar
- 2 tsp. Dijon mustard
- 2 tbsp. raisins
- Pinch of sugar

**Methods:**

1. Heat oven to 200 °C.
2. Roast shallots for 10 minutes with 1 tsp. oil in a baking tray, stirring midway.
3. Combine oil, vinegar, mustard, some seasoning, raisins, and sugar.
4. Combine oil, almonds, a pinch of sea salt, and paprika in a roasting pot.
5. Coat the kale with seasoning and 1 tsp. vegetable oil.
6. Add kale to shallot tray.
7. Put the almonds on the lower shelf.
8. Roast for 7 minutes, turning kale midway.
9. Put ham on the plates.
10. Add shallots, kale, and celery into the dressing.
11. Add the mixture on top of ham.
12. Serve with roasted almonds and cheese.

**Patatas Bravas**

Main Ingredient: Potatoes

Total time: 1 hour 10 minutes

Serving: 4 persons

**Ingredients:**

- 5 tbsp. olive oil
- 750g Maris Piper potatoes, cut into chunks
- 1 onion, chopped
- 400g tin tomatoes, chopped
- 3 garlic cloves, crushed
- 3 vine tomatoes, chopped
- 1 tbsp. sherry vinegar
- ½ tsp. dried chili flakes
- 1 tsp. caster sugar
- Flat-leaf parsley, chopped
- ½ tsp. sweet smoked paprika

**Method:**

1. Heat salted water in a large pan.
2. Add in the potatoes and cook for 3 minutes.
3. Drain potatoes.
4. Heat the oven to 200°C.
5. Add potatoes with 3 tbsp. olive oil on a baking tray.
6. Roast for 40-50 minutes, tossing midway.
7. Cook the garlic and onions in 2 tbsp. oil for 15-20 minutes on low.
8. Add the remaining ingredients and seasonings.
9. Cook on low for 20 minutes.
10. Sprinkle salt on potatoes.
11. Serve with sauce and sprinkled with parsley.

# Crispy Wonton Pea and Ricotta Ravioli

Main Ingredient: Peas

Total time: 40 minutes

Serving: 4 persons

**Ingredients:**

- 1 cup green peas
- 1 cup ricotta cheese
- 1 egg
- Tomato sauce or butter sauce
- Zest from 1 lemon
- 1/4 cup Parmigiano Reggiano, grated
- 1 tsp. thyme leaves, chopped
- Ground black pepper, to taste
- 1/2 tsp. Kosher salt
- 40 wonton wrappers

**Method:**

1. Combine the peas, ricotta cheese, egg, lemon zest, Parmigiano Reggiano, salt thyme, and pepper in a bowl.
2. Put 1 tbsp. stuffing in the middle of the wonton wrappers.
3. Brush water on the edges.
4. Put a second wrapper on top.
5. Seal the edges.
6. Fry raviolis over medium-high heat for 30 seconds on each side.

7.  Serve hot with butter sauce or tomato sauce.

## Blistered Padrón Peppers

Main Ingredient: Peppers

Total time: 10 minutes

Serving: 4 persons

**Ingredients:**

- 3 tbsp. olive oil
- 1 lemon juiced
- 3 cups Padrón peppers, rinsed and dried
- Maldon salt

**Method:**

1.  Sauté Padrón peppers for about 5-7 minutes in oil, turning midway.
2.  Remove peppers from the oil.
3.  Season with salt and lemon juice and serve.

## Zanahorias Aliñadas

Main Ingredient: Carrots

Total time: 4 hours 35 minutes

Serving: 4-6 persons

**Ingredients:**

- 2 garlic cloves, peeled
- 17 1/2 oz. carrots (6-7), peeled
- 1 tbsp. dried oregano

- 1/2 cup water
- 1 tsp. sweet paprika
- 2 tsp. cumin seeds
- 1/2 cup sherry vinegar

**Methods:**

1. Fill a pot with water and salt and bring it to a boil.
2. Add the carrots and cook until soft.
3. Remove the hot water and replace it with cold water.
4. Cut carrots into 1/3 inch pieces when cool.
5. Put carrots in a jar.
6. Mash garlic with cumin seeds, oregano, and paprika in a mortar and pestle.
7. Add the mix to the jar along with the carrots.
8. Add water and vinegar.
9. Cover the jar and refrigerate for 4 hours.
10. Take the carrots out of the jar.
11. Sprinkle with olive oil, salt, and freshly chopped parsley and serve.

---

**Lemony Skewered Artichokes**

Main Ingredient: Artichoke

Total time: 1 hour

Serving: 4 persons

**Ingredients:**

- 4 sprigs of fresh thyme
- 1 lemon

- 10 slices of mixed cured meat (higher-welfare)
- 1 tbsp. runny honey
- 6 jarred artichokes
- Extra virgin olive oil
- 50g feta cheese

**Method:**

1. Stick a knife in the lemon carefully and put it in a pan.
2. Add boiling water and boil for 40 minutes.
3. Remove the lemon carefully and set it aside to cool.
4. Cut the lemon in half.
5. Take out the flesh of the lemon.
6. Add the flesh with honey, thyme leaves, and oil.
7. Season with black pepper and sea salt.
8. Slice the artichoke in half and place the pieces on a griddle.
9. Cook for a few minutes on each side.
10. Cut the artichoke pieces in half.
11. Drizzle artichokes with dressing.
12. Cut the feta cheese.
13. Slice the cured meats into long strips.
14. Roll the strips.
15. Add the strips to skewers, along with dressed artichokes, and serve.

## Marinated Olive and Cheese Ring

Main Ingredient: Olive

Total time: 35 minutes

Serving: 16 persons

**Ingredients:**

- (10 oz.) 1 pack sharp white cheddar cheese, 1/4-inch slices
- (8 oz.) 1 pack cream cheese, cold
- 1/3 cup olives (pimiento-stuffed)
- 1/4 cup balsamic vinegar
- 1/3 cup Greek olives, pitted
- 1/4 cup olive oil
- 1 tbsp. basil, minced
- 1 tbsp. fresh parsley, minced
- 2 garlic cloves, minced
- Slices of toasted French bread baguette
- (2 oz.) 1 jar pimiento strips, chopped

**Method:**

1. Slice the cream cheese in half lengthwise.
2. Cut the pieces into 1/4-inch slices.
3. Put cheese in a circle upright with alternating slices of cream cheese and cheddar cheese on a serving plate.
4. Arrange olives in the middle.
5. Whisk oil, vinegar, parsley, garlic, and basil until blended in a small bowl.

6. Drizzle the mix over olives and cheeses.

7. Sprinkle pimientos on top.

8. Cover and chill for 8 hours.

9. Serve along with baguette slices.

## Jalapeño Popper Fritters

Main Ingredient: Jalapeno

Total time: 40 minutes

Serving: 3-4 persons

**Ingredients:**

- 20g cheddar cheese or Monterey Jack, grated
- 100g cream cheese (full-fat)
- 1 tsp. fresh chives, chopped
- 12 pancetta slices, halved
- 12 jalapeño chilies, deseeded and halved lengthways
- 3 tbsp. plain flour
- 6-8 tbsp. panko breadcrumbs
- 2 medium eggs, beaten
- Lime wedges
- Soured cream

**Method:**

1. Mix the grated cheese and chives in a bowl.

2. Fill the jalapeño halves with the above mixture.

3. Wrap each jalapeño half in half pancetta slice.

4. Put the beaten eggs, flour, and panko breadcrumbs in different bowls.

5. Roll jalapeños in flour.

6. Coat with egg.

7. Roll in breadcrumbs.

8. Let chill for 30 minutes on a baking sheet covered lightly.

9. Fry in batches for 2-3 minutes on both sides

10. Serve jalapeños with lime wedges and sour cream.

## Baby Potatoes in Sea Salt with Herb Salsa

Main Ingredient: Potato

Total time: 55 minutes

Serving: 4 persons

**Ingredients:**

- 1 tbsp. sea salt
- 600g baby new potatoes
- 3 small handfuls of herbs (basil, mint, and parsley), leaves picked
- 6 tbsp. olive oil
- 2-3 tbsp. white wine vinegar
- 2 garlic cloves, crushed

**Method:**

1. Pour water into a deep saucepan and add salt to it.

2. Add the baby potatoes.

3. Bring the water to a boil and cook for 40 minutes or until potatoes get a salty crust.

4. Cut the herbs finely, and mix with the oil, vinegar, and garlic.

5. Season the mixture to taste.

6. Drizzle the herb salsa over the potatoes and serve.

## Pan con Tomate with Garrotxa Cheese

Main Ingredient: Tomato

Total time: 20 minutes

Serving: 2-3 persons

**Ingredients:**

- Extra-virgin olive oil
- 8 1/2-inch ciabatta slices
- 2 garlic cloves, halved horizontally
- Kosher salt
- 4 tomatoes, halved horizontally
- Shaved Garrotxa cheese
- Pepper

**Methods:**

1. Preheat the oven to 191°C.
2. Put oil on one side of bread slices.
3. Bake for 10 minutes with the oiled side up.
4. Rub garlic cloves on the toasts.
5. Rub tomato halves on the toasts.
6. Season the toasts with pepper and salt.
7. Put cheese on the top.
8. Drizzle over olive oil and serve.

# Tortilla Espanola

Main Ingredient: Potato

Total time: 30 minutes

Serving: 4 persons

## Ingredients:

- 1 pound red potatoes, sliced
- 1/3 cup olive oil
- 1/2 white onion, sliced
- 1/2 tsp. salt
- 6 eggs

## Method:

1. Fry onions and potatoes in a skillet according to your thickness preference for the Tortilla Espanola.
2. Toss around the vegetables until they start to brown.
3. Remove the onions and potatoes.
4. Beat the eggs with salt in a bowl.
5. Put the vegetables back in the skillet.
6. Add the beaten eggs on top.
7. Cook for 3-4 minutes over low heat, shaking midway.
8. Put the skillet in the oven.
9. Broil for 3-4 minutes.
10. Cut it into wedges and serve.

# Fried Stuffed Olives with Tomato Sauce

Main Ingredient: Olive

Total time: 30 minutes

Serving: 4 persons

**Ingredients:**

- 354g black olives jar
- 500 g passata
- 65g feta cheese
- 40g plain flour
- 1 tbsp. capers
- 2 large eggs
- 1-liter vegetable oil
- 200g breadcrumbs
- Sprigs of fresh oregano
- Extra virgin olive oil
- Pinch of dried chili

**Method:**

1. Add passata to a big dish.
2. Wash it and remove stones.
3. Add olives.
4. Soak mixture for 1 hour.
5. Beat the capers and feta together to form a paste.
6. Take the olives out of the passata.
7. Make balls out of the feta and capers mixture.
8. Insert the balls in the olives.

9. Roll the stuffed olives in flour.

10. Coat them with eggs.

11. Roll them in breadcrumbs.

12. Deep fry stuffed olives over medium-high heat in a deep pan until golden.

13. Put the leftover passata with dried chili and oregano leaves.

14. Add seasoning.

15. Cook on medium-high heat for 4-5 minutes.

16. Add extra virgin olive oil.

17. Serve olives with a glass of wine and sauce.

## Heirloom Tomato Galette with Pecorino

Main Ingredient: Tomato

Total time: 35 minutes

Serving: 6 persons

**Ingredients:**

- 1 tsp. baking powder
- 1 cup all-purpose flour
- 3/4 tsp. kosher salt, divided
- 1/2 cup butter, unsalted, cold, and cubed
- 2 cups cherry tomatoes, halved
- 1/2 cup sour cream
- 3 oz. pecorino Romano cheese, sliced

**Method:**

1. Mix baking powder, flour, and 1/2 tsp. salt.

2. Add butter and mix until the mixture is crumbly.

3. Add sour cream.

4. Shape the dough into a ball.

5. Roll the ball into a disk.

6. Refrigerate for 2 hours, covered.

7. Sprinkle tomatoes with remaining salt and set aside for 15 minutes.

8. Preheat oven to 218°C.

9. Make a circle of about 12-inches out of the dough.

10. Put cheese slices on the dough, leaving 2 inches around the edges.

11. Top tomatoes with cheese.

12. Fold the edges of the crust over a bit of filling.

13. Bake for about 25 minutes until golden.

14. Set aside for 10 minutes.

15. Slice and serve.

---

## Pickled Pepper and Sherry Croquetas

Main Ingredient: Tomato

Total time: 1 hour 10 minutes

Serving: 3-4 persons

**Ingredients:**

- 1 shallot, chopped
- 3 tbsp. olive oil
- 100g pickled guindilla peppers, sliced
- 60ml vegetable stock

- 110g plain flour, more for dusting
- 280ml whole milk
- 40ml dry sherry (fino)
- A pinch of nutmeg, grated
- 2 medium eggs, beaten
- 2 liters sunflower oil for frying
- 60g breadcrumbs

**Method:**

1. Cook shallots for about 10 minutes over medium heat in a saucepan.
2. Put in the peppers and cook for 1 minute.
3. Add 50g flour.
4. Cook for 5 minutes.
5. Turn the heat low.
6. Mix the milk and stock.
7. Slowly add the mix to the saucepan stirring constantly.
8. Season with pepper, salt, and nutmeg.
9. Add sherry and mix.
10. Spread béchamel sauce on a plate and refrigerate for 1 hour, covered.
11. Put the remaining eggs, flour, and breadcrumbs in different bowls.
12. Make balls out of the sauce with floured hands.
13. Coat with flour.
14. Roll in eggs.
15. Coat with breadcrumbs.

16. Refrigerate for 30 minutes.

17. Heat oil to 175°C in a deep saucepan.

18. Fry croquetas for 2-3 minutes until golden.

19. Serve with sauces.

## Goat's cheese, Fennel and Roasted Red Pepper Tart

Main Ingredient: Fennel

Total time: 1 hour 20 minutes

Serving: 8 persons

**Ingredients:**

- 3 tbsp. olive oil
- 375g sheet puff pastry (all-butter)
- 1 red onion, chopped
- 1 Romano pepper, deseeded and chopped
- 1 fennel bulb, chopped with core removed
- 2 garlic cloves, crushed
- 200ml double cream
- 2 eggs and 1 egg yolk
- 100ml milk
- 100g goat's cheese
- ½ tsp. sweet paprika
- Caperberries
- 12 olives, pitted

**Method:**

1. Spread the pastry with a roller to the thickness of a coin.

2. Use a 20 x 3.5cm loose-based deep tart tin.

3. Put the pastry at the bottom.

4. Fork the base, cover, and refrigerate for 30 minutes.

5. Pre-heat oven to 200°C.

6. Fill the pastry with baking beans over baking parchment paper.

7. Bake for 15 minutes.

8. Cook the pastry without the beans for another 8-10 minutes.

9. Lower the oven to 180°C.

10. Cook fennel, onion, and pepper for 15 minutes over medium-high heat.

11. Add the garlic.

12. Cook for some minutes.

13. Mix cream, paprika, seasonings, eggs, and milk.

14. Add the vegetable mixture onto the tart.

15. Top with olives and cheese.

16. Add eggs on the top.

17. Bake for 20-25 minutes.

18. Let cool and cut into slices.

19. Serve with caper berries.

## Fingerling Papas Bravas with Smoky Aioli

Main Ingredient: Potato

Total time: 40 minutes

Serving: 8 persons

**Ingredients:**

- Kosher salt
- 3 pounds fingerling potatoes
- 2 large egg yolks
- 2 tbsp. fresh lemon juice
- 1 small garlic clove, mashed
- 1/2 tsp. lemon zest, grated
- 1 tsp. sweet smoked paprika
- Maldon sea salt
- 1 cup vegetable oil
- 2 tbsp. flat-leaf parsley, finely chopped

**Method:**

1. Boil potatoes with salt for 10 minutes.
2. Cut each potato vertically.
3. Mix egg yolks, lemon juice, and zest, and garlic in a bowl.
4. Add the vegetable oil slowly, stirring constantly.
5. Add paprika and kosher salt.
6. Fry the potatoes at 176°C for 5 minutes and remove.
7. Sprinkle Maldon salt and parsley on the potatoes.
8. Serve with the smoky aioli.

---

**Pan-Fried Cauliflower**

Main Ingredient: Cauliflower

Total time: 30 minutes

Serving: 6 persons

## Ingredients:

- Vegetable oil
- 1 medium head cauliflower
- 3 large eggs
- 1 tsp. paprika
- 1 1/3 cups bread crumbs, dried
- Kosher salt

## Method:

1. Slice the cauliflower into bite-sized pieces.
2. Steam the cauliflower pieces for 5 minutes.
3. Put the cauliflower into cold water.
4. Beat the eggs in a bowl.
5. Mix breadcrumbs and paprika in another.
6. Coat the florets with egg.
7. Roll them into breadcrumbs.
8. Fry the florets in oil for 2 minutes at 176°C.
9. Season with salt and serve.

---

### Stuffed Cuke Snacks

Main Ingredient: Cucumber

Total time: 30 minutes

Serving: 3-4 persons

### Ingredients:

- 3 oz. cream cheese softened
- 1 large cucumber

- 1 tbsp. blue cheese, crumbled
- 1 tsp. fresh dill, minced
- 2 tsp. fresh parsley, minced
- 1 tsp. onion, grated
- 20-26 pimiento strips,
- Dill sprigs

**Method:**

1. Cut 1 inch from the bottom and top of each cucumber.
2. Cut the cucumbers in half.
3. Discard seeds.
4. Keep the cucumber on a paper towel with the cut side down for 10 minutes.
5. Combine parsley, cheeses, onion, and dill.
6. Put the mixture into cucumber halves.
7. Combine the halves.
8. Wrap the cucumber in plastic.
9. Refrigerate for 3-4 hours.
10. Cut into half-inch slices.
11. Serve with pimiento strips and dill.

# Chilled Pea Soup Shooters

Main Ingredient: Pea

Total time: 30 minutes

Serving: 3-4 persons

**Ingredients:**

- 1 cup chicken broth
- (16 oz.) 1 package frozen peas, thawed
- 1/4 cup fresh mint, minced
- 1 tsp. ground cumin
- 1 tbsp. lime juice
- 1-1/2 cups plain yogurt
- 1/4 tsp. salt

Curried Crab

- 4 tsp. lime juice
- 2 tbsp. fresh mint, minced
- 4 tsp. canola oil
- 1/8 tsp. salt
- 2 tsp. red curry paste
- 1 cup lump crabmeat, drained

**Method:**

- Blend the broth, peas, mint, cumin, salt, and lime juice.
- Add yogurt and refrigerate for 1 hour.
- Combine the lime juice, mint, oil, salt, and curry paste.
- Add in crabmeat.

- Pour chilled soup into shot glasses.
- Top with crab mixture and serve.

## Zucchini Patties with Dill Dip

Main Ingredient: Zucchini

Total time: 35 minutes

Serving: 3-4 persons

**Ingredients:**

- 2 tbsp. fresh dill, minced
- 3/4 cup sour cream
- 1 tsp. lemon juice
- 1/8 tsp. pepper
- 1/8 tsp. salt
- 2-1/2 cups zucchini, shredded
- 1 tsp. seafood seasoning
- 1 cup bread crumbs, seasoned
- 1/4 tsp. garlic powder
- 2 tbsp. butter, melted
- 1 egg, lightly beaten
- 1 carrot, chopped
- 1/4 cup all-purpose flour
- 1/4 cup onion, finely chopped
- 1/2 cup canola oil

**Method:**

1. Combine the first five ingredients.

2. Cover and chill.
3. Pat dry zucchini.
4. Combine the seafood seasoning, bread crumbs, and garlic powder.
5. Stir in butter and egg.
6. Add the onion, carrot, and zucchini.
7. Make 24 patties out of zucchini mixture.
8. Coat patties with flour.
9. Fry patties from each side for 3-4 minutes.
10. Serve patties with dip.

The above-mentioned recipes for some tapa dishes focused on fish, meat, and vegetables. Now let me introduce you briefly to the Spanish Cuisine and some of its prominent dishes.

# Chapter 4: Famous Spanish Dish Recipes

Traditional Spanish cuisine is unpretentious and down-to-earth food focused on locally available ingredients or on regional crops. The same preparation techniques and ingredients are used to make several dishes today as they were two or three hundred years ago.

Mountains run in many directions across Spain, serving as natural obstacles to interaction and, until the last half of the 20th century, rendering transportation challenging. This is only one of the reasons why cooking is so distinctive from region to region. Another is the fact that, by uniting several small kingdoms, each with their own customs, Spain was founded. Other dishes were drawn from European and American influences and tailored to the tastes of Spain. Now let me introduce you to some dishes that are famous all-around Spain.

### Gazpacho

Main Ingredient: Tomato

Total time: 15 minutes

Serving: 4 persons

**Ingredients:**

- 6-7 medium tomatoes
- 1 green Italian pepper, de-seeded and sliced
- ½ small white onion, chopped
- 1 clove of garlic, chopped
- 1/4 cup extra virgin olive oil
- A splash of red wine vinegar

- 1 cucumber, peeled
- A pinch or two of salt
- Green apple, diced
- Cucumber, diced
- Onion, diced
- Croutons
- Pepper, diced
- Hard-boiled eggs

**Method:**

1. Wash and dry the vegetables.
2. Cut each tomato into 4 pieces.
3. Blend tomatoes.
4. Add the sliced pepper, onion, half cucumber sliced, and garlic.
5. Add salt and vinegar.
6. Add olive oil slowly.
7. Refrigerate and serve cold with the last 6 ingredients as toppings.

---

**Paella Valenciana**

Main Ingredient: Rabbit

Total time: 2 hours

Serving: 8 persons

**Ingredients:**

- (4 pound) ½ whole chicken, chopped into 6 pieces
- 1 tbsp. olive oil

- (2 pound) ½ rabbit, cut into pieces
- 1 tomato, chopped
- 1 head garlic, peeled
- (15.5 oz.) 1 can butter beans
- (10 oz.) ½ package frozen green beans
- (10 oz.) ½ package frozen green peas
- Salt to taste
- 1 pinch of saffron threads
- 1 tsp. mild paprika, or to taste
- 1 pinch thyme, dried
- 4 cups white rice, uncooked
- 1 pinch rosemary, dried

**Method:**

1. Put a paella pan coated with olive oil on medium-high heat.
2. Add the rabbit, chicken, and garlic.
3. Cook until browned.
4. Add the butter beans, tomato, green beans, and peas.
5. Season with paprika.
6. Fill the pan with water.
7. Bring the mixture to a boil.
8. Cook on low for 1 hour.
9. Season with salt and saffron.
10. Sprinkle rosemary and thyme.
11. Add the rice.
12. Cover.

13. Cook on low for 20 minutes and serve.

---

**Cocido Madrileño**

Main Ingredient: Chickpeas

Total time: 4-6 hours

Serving: 4 persons

**Ingredients:**

- 300g beef black pudding
- 250g chickpeas
- ¼ chicken
- 100g black pudding with onion
- 100g streaky bacon
- 100g spicy sausage
- 4 marrow bones (5 cm long)
- 50g cured ham end
- 1 kg cabbage, chopped
- 2 carrots
- Salt to taste
- 4 medium potatoes, peeled and halved
- 1 onion
- 1 clove of garlic
- 1 turnip
- 100g stick noodles

**For the mix:**

- 75g breadcrumbs

- 2 eggs, beaten
- 2 cloves of garlic, chopped
- Olive oil
- 2 tsp. finely-chopped parsley
- Salt

**Method:**

1. Soak chickpeas overnight with salt in warm water.
2. Put the bacon, meat, ham, and washed bones in an earthenware dish.
3. Add 4 liters of water.
4. Boil the mix.
5. Add the chickpeas, carrot, turnip, and onion.
6. Cook on low for two hours and forty minutes.
7. Add potatoes and salt and cook for 20 minutes.
8. Boil cabbage for 30 minutes separately.
9. Fry cabbage with garlic.
10. Cook the black pudding and spicy sausage separately.
11. Mix eggs, breadcrumbs, garlic, salt, and parsley.
12. Make balls from the mixture and fry until brown.
13. Add to broth and boil the mixture.
14. Cook the noodles in the broth for 5 minutes.
15. Serve noodles and soup with the chick peas mixture, fried tomatoes, balls, and meat pieces.

## Churros with Chocolate Sauce

Main Ingredient: Flour

Total time: 40 minutes

Serving: 4 persons

**Ingredients:**

- 2 tbsp. sugar
- 1 tbsp. vanilla sugar
- 1/3 tsp. salt
- 2 tbsp. butter
- 1 cup all-purpose flour
- 4 cups refined coconut oil
- 3 tbsp. light brown sugar
- ¾ tsp. cinnamon

For the chocolate sauce:

- ¼ cup heavy cream
- 2 oz. dark chocolate (70%), chopped

**Method:**

1. Mix cinnamon and sugar on a plate.
2. Boil sugar, water, butter, and salt and remove.
3. Add the flour.
4. Make dough of the mixture.
5. Put the dough mix in a piping bag with a star-shaped tip.
6. Fry churros for 4 minutes turnip midway.
7. Coat the churros in cinnamon sugar.
8. Heat cream.
9. Add the chocolate.
10. Serve churros with the sauce.

## Traditional Spanish Pisto

Main Ingredient: Eggplants

Total time: 35 minutes

Serving: 4 persons

**Ingredients:**

- 3 zucchinis, diced
- 2 red bell peppers, diced
- 2 green bell peppers, diced
- 4 onions, diced
- 3 purple eggplants, peeled and diced
- 2 pounds ripe tomatoes, peeled and diced
- 5 garlic cloves, diced
- Thyme rosemary
- Fresh oregano
- 1 tsp. cumin
- 1 tsp. refined sugar
- Salt and pepper to taste
- Extra virgin olive oil

**Method:**

1. Sprinkle eggplant with kosher salt. Let it stay for 10 minutes.
2. Cook onions with salt on medium heat until transparent.
3. Cover and cook until tender.
4. Fry peppers for 10 minutes.

5. Cook the washed eggplants until transparent.

6. Cover and cook until tender.

7. Mix all the vegetables.

8. Add seasonings.

9. Sauté garlic in a pan.

10. Add tomatoes and cook for 20 minutes, stirring constantly.

11. Add the sugar and salt.

12. Mix vegetables with the tomato sauce.

13. Cook for 10 minutes and serve.

## Cordero Asado

Main Ingredient: Lamb

Total time: 2 hours 10 minutes

Serving: 8-10 persons

**Ingredients:**

- 6 oz. vegetable shortening, melted
- 1/2 suckling lamb (9-11 lbs.)
- Salt to taste
- 10 small potatoes, peeled and halved

**Method:**

1. Heat vegetable shortening to melt it.

2. Pre-heat oven to 204°C.

3. Cut the excess fat off the lamb.

4. Coat lamb and potatoes with salt and melted shortening.

5. Roast lamb until tender, coating it and potatoes with shortening occasionally.

6. Let sit for 10 minutes and serve.

---

## Spanish Stuffed Aubergine

Main Ingredient: Eggplant

Total time: 1 hour 40 minutes

Serving: 4 persons

**Ingredients:**

- 8 small aubergines (eggplant), 12cm long
- Olive oil
- 1 onion, chopped
- 1 red pepper, seeded and diced
- 2 garlic cloves, chopped
- 1 tsp. ground cumin
- 200g courgettes, diced
- 400g plum tomatoes, skinned and chopped
- ½ tsp. chili flakes, dried

**For Migas Topping**

- 2 garlic cloves, chopped
- 150g day-old crustless sourdough, pieces
- 2 shallots, diced
- 1/2 tbsp. lemon juice
- Few thyme sprig leaves, chopped
- 3 tbsp. olive oil

**Method:**

1. Pre-heat the oven to 180°C.

2. Coat the bread with shallots, garlic, and thyme.

3. Bake the bread until the bread is golden.

4. Blend the bread to make breadcrumbs.

5. Add olive oil and lemon juice.

6. Using a skewer, make holes on the aubergines.

7. Bake for 30 minutes.

8. Fry red pepper and onion in oil, covered on low for 7-8 minutes.

9. Add the garlic, dried chili, and cumin and cook for 1 minute.

10. Cut aubergines in half.

11. Take out the flesh and chop.

12. Add aubergine to the onion pan.

13. Cook for some minutes.

14. Add courgettes and salt.

15. Cook for 4 minutes.

16. Add 150ml water and the tomatoes for 10 minutes.

17. Put pisto in the aubergine shells.

18. Sprinkle over breadcrumbs.

19. Bake for 15 minutes and serve.

## Sangria

Main Ingredient: Pear

Total time: 1 hour 10 minutes

Serving: 6 persons

**Ingredients:**

- 2 pears, chopped
- 2 oranges, chopped
- 2 lemons, 1 juiced, and 1 chopped
- 3 tbsp. caster sugar
- 200g red berries, chopped
- 1 tsp. cinnamon
- 100ml Spanish brandy
- 750ml light red wine
- 300ml sparkling water

**Method:**

1. Add cinnamon and sugar to the fruit and mix.
2. Cover and refrigerate for 1 hour.
3. Put ice in a big jug.
4. Add the fruit mixture, brandy, and wine to the jug.
5. Top with sparkling water and serve.

---

**Turron de Alicante**

Main Ingredient: Almond

Total time: 1 hour 15 minutes

Serving: 25 persons

**Ingredients:**

- 200g sugar
- 200g honey

- 300g whole blanched almonds
- 1 egg white

**Method:**

1. Toast almonds at 190°C until golden brown on both sides.
2. Melt sugar and honey over low heat in a pan over low heat.
3. Beat the egg white.
4. Add in sugar mixture slowly.
5. Cook the mixture in the pan over low heat, stirring constantly.
6. Take a little candy and put it in water.
7. If it gets hard, stop cooking the candy.
8. Add almonds and mix.
9. Put in silicone molds between wafer sheets.
10. Cool and serve.

---

### Fabada

Main Ingredient: Beans

Total time: 11 hours 5 minutes

Serving: 8 persons

**Ingredients:**

- ¼ pound salt pork
- 1 pound dried lima beans
- 10 cups water
- 8 oz. serrano ham, 1/4-inch cubes

- ½ tsp. saffron threads, crushed
- 8 oz. Spanish chorizo sausage without casing, cut into 1/2-inch thick
- 1 bay leaf
- 8 oz. blood sausage, cut into 1/2-inch thick

**Method:**

1. Soak beans in hot water overnight.
2. Fill half a Dutch oven with water.
3. Boil the water.
4. Add in salt pork, and boil for 5 minutes.
5. Remove water.
6. Put the drained beans in the Dutch oven.
7. Boil 10 cups of water in the oven, discarding the foam.
8. Add salt pork, saffron, and diced ham.
9. Cook on low for 5 minutes.
10. Add the morcilla sausages and chorizo.
11. Cook for 5 minutes.
12. Add in the bay leaf.
13. Cover, reduce heat, and cook for 2-3 hours.
14. Let it rest and serve.

---

**Salmorejo**

Main Ingredient: Tomato

Total time: 25 minutes

Serving: 4 persons

**Ingredients:**

- 1 baguette
- 8 tomatoes
- 1 cup extra virgin olive oil
- A splash of red wine vinegar
- 1 garlic clove
- A pinch of salt
- Serrano ham, sliced
- 2 hard-boiled eggs

**Method:**

1. Make two cross-cuts at the bottom of each tomato.
2. Add tomatoes for 40-60 seconds in salted boiling water.
3. Put tomatoes in cold water instantly.
4. Take out the flesh of the tomatoes and blend it.
5. Add torn baguette in the tomatoes.
6. Let it stay for 5 minutes.
7. Add salt, vinegar, and garlic.
8. Blend well.
9. Add olive oil slowly during blending.
10. Add 1 hard-boiled egg.
11. Serve cold with sliced ham and 1 diced egg.

### Huevos Rotos

Main Ingredient: Potatoes

Total time: 40 minutes

Serving: 4 persons

**Ingredients:**

- 4 eggs
- 4 potatoes, sliced
- 1 large onion, sliced
- Serrano ham, thin slices
- ½ cup green pepper, sliced
- 1 link Spanish chorizo, cured and diced
- 1 tbsp. parsley
- Salt and pepper
- 5 garlic cloves, minced
- Extra virgin olive oil

**Method:**

1. Cook onions over medium-high heat.
2. Add the potatoes.
3. Add garlic, peppers, and parsley.
4. Reduce heat and cover.
5. Cook for about 30 minutes, stirring three times midway.
6. Crack the eggs on the potatoes.
7. Reduce heat more.
8. Cover and cook until egg whites set.
9. Slit the yolks and remove the pan.
10. Brown the chorizo in a pan.
11. Season with pepper and salt.
12. Serve potatoes with chorizo and ham slices.

# Cod 'al pil-pil'

Main Ingredient: Cod

Total time: 50 minutes

Serving: 4 persons

## Ingredients:

- ¼ liter olive oil
- 1 chili pepper, sliced
- 4 pieces of salted cod, sliced from the side
- 6 garlic cloves, sliced

## Method:

1. Soak the cod for 36 hours, changing water 3 times in between.
2. Remove the bones, scales and dry.
3. Fry garlic in an earthenware pot on low and remove.
4. Fry cod for 10 minutes on low.
5. Place another earthenware dish over a flame and add some of the oil from the cod.
6. Transfer some oil from the pot to another.
7. Add the fish to the pot with the skin down.
8. Shake the pot from side to side gently, slowly adding the oil.
9. Serve cod with chili pepper and garlic.

# Spanish Torrijas

Main Ingredient: Bread

Total time: 5 hours 5 minutes

Serving: 3-4 persons

**Ingredients:**

- A day-old bread, sliced (2.5cm)
- 1-liter milk
- 3-4 eggs
- Orange and lemon peel
- Extra virgin olive oil
- Sugar
- 1 cinnamon stick
- Cinnamon powder

**Method:**

1. Add pieces from orange and lemon peel and cinnamon to the milk.
2. Soak the bread in milk for 4 hours.
3. Beat eggs.
4. Dip the bread in eggs.
5. Deep fry the bread slices 2-3 minutes on each side.
6. Coat the bread in a sugar mixture and serve.

---

**Ajo Blanco Soup**

Main Ingredient: Almond

Total time: 2 hours 10 minutes

Serving: 6 persons

**Ingredients:**

- 720ml cold water
- 6 oz. blanched almonds
- 1-2 garlic cloves

- Kosher salt
- 225g fresh, crustless rustic bread, 1-inch cubes
- 7ml sherry vinegar
- Crushed toasted almonds, green seedless grapes, and sliced mint leaves
- 22ml extra-virgin olive oil

**Method:**

1. Blend almonds, water, and garlic.
2. Add bread, salt, and vinegar.
3. Strain the mixture.
4. Refrigerate for 2 hours.
5. Serve with mint, almonds, grapes, and drizzled olive oil.

---

### Tarta de Santiago

Main Ingredient: Egg

Total time: 45 minutes

Serving: 5-6 persons

**Ingredients:**

- 125gm of sugar flour
- 1 egg
- Cinnamon

**For the filling:**

- 250gm sugar
- 4 eggs
- 250gm almonds, ground

- Cinnamon icing sugar
- Lemon rind

**Method:**

1. Beat the egg with 1 tbsp. water, little cinnamon, and sugar.
2. Add flour gradually.
3. Roll out the dough.
4. Put it on a greased tin.
5. Beat the sugar, lemon rind, and eggs.
6. Add cinnamon and almonds.
7. Add filling to the tin.
8. Bake for 25-30 minutes at 180°C.
9. Place a cardboard St. James cross in the center of the cake and dust it.
10. Serve.

---

### Spanish Rice Pudding

Main Ingredient: Rice

Total time: 45 minutes

Serving: 4 persons

**Ingredients:**

- 1 1/2 cups medium-grain rice
- 3 cups water
- 2 cups whole milk
- 2 oz. unsalted butter
- 1/2 cup sugar

- 1/2 lemon peel
- 1 cinnamon stick

**Methods:**

1. Boil rice on medium-low heat for 10 minutes.

2. Boil milk and sugar on medium-low heat.

3. Add the butter, drained rice, lemon peel, and cinnamon stick.

4. Cook for 15 to 20 minutes.

5. Remove lemon peel and cinnamon stick.

6. Top with ground cinnamon.

7. Cool for 10-25 minutes and serve.

# Conclusion

Without comprehending the food of Spain, it is absolutely impossible to understand Spain. A Spaniard's food is a source of pride, a way of living; it is fundamental to their identity. Without a doubt, the principal feature of contemporary Spain is its geographical richness, which has given rise to such a versatile cuisine.

A big part of Spanish cuisine is tapas. Spain draws a diverse audience by holding the tradition of tapas alive and evolving. In addition, the tapas movement continues to have a positive impact on locals who attach great value to customs. This book containing not only tapa recipes but also famous Spanish recipes is a gesture of love for food.